Clothed in Humility:

30 Days Learning to Walk Humbly with God

I0107652

By Dr. Robert Clayton, DMin • DBA

Scripture quotations are from the NASB® (New American Standard Bible®), Copyright ©1995 by The Lockman Foundation. Used by permission. All rights reserved.

Cover design by Dr. Robert M. Clayton
Interior design by Dr. Robert M. Clayton

ISBN: 979-8-9943368-0-9
First Edition

Printed in the United States of America
* * *

Introduction: Why Humility? Why Now?

Pride is subtle, relentless, and deadly. It was the first sin to fracture heaven (Isaiah 14:13-15), the root of humanity's rebellion (Genesis 3:5), and remains the silent saboteur of spiritual vitality today. Left unchecked, pride poisons our relationships, distorts our view of God, and renders our faith performative rather than transformative.

Yet Scripture offers a better way. Again and again, God declares, "I oppose the proud, but give grace to the humble" (James 4:6, NASB95). Humility is not self-hatred—it is self-forgetfulness in the presence of divine glory. It is the gateway to wisdom (Proverbs 11:2), spiritual rest (Matthew 11:29), and Christlike maturity (Philippians 2:5-8).

This devotional exists to lead you on a 30-day journey to cultivate humility and confront pride through daily engagement with God's Word. These aren't academic reflections; they are soul-level calls to surrender. The goal is not merely behavior modification, but spiritual reformation by the grace of God.

How to Use This Devotional

Each daily entry contains:

- A Scripture Focus (NASB95): A key passage on humility or pride.

- Exegetical Insight: A concise explanation of the biblical text in context.

- Practical Application: A challenge to live out the truth in daily life.

- Reflection Prompt: A journaling question or thought to personalize the day's theme.

You may want to keep a journal alongside this devotional, either using the provided space or your own separate journal. Whether with pen and paper or digitally, give yourself space to respond honestly to God's Spirit as He convicts, encourages, and shapes your heart.

Expectations and Posture

Do not expect to finish this devotional unchanged. Expect the Holy Spirit to confront hidden areas of pride. Expect moments of deep repentance. Expect joy in rediscovering the gentleness and strength of humility. Expect Jesus to be exalted in your thinking, your relationships, and your self-understanding.

This journey will not be easy. But it will be worth it. Every page is an invitation to "walk humbly with your God" (Micah 6:8) and to become more like Christ (gentle, lowly, and full of grace).

So take a breath. Slow down. Open your Bible, open your heart, and begin.

The way up is down. Let's walk low together.

Day 1: Walking Humbly with God

Scripture (NASB95):

He has told you, O man, what is good; And what does the LORD require of you but to do justice, to love kindness, and to walk humbly with your God?

Micah 6:8

Insight:

In this verse, the prophet Micah summarizes God's requirements for His people. Rather than grand offerings or proud religious show, God desires a life marked by justice, mercy, and a humble walk with Him. This verse is similar theology to Deuteronomy 10:12. True humility means living in obedient fellowship with God, acknowledging His Lordship, and aligning our attitudes with His character.

Application:

Embrace a lifestyle of "walking humbly," that is, your lifestyle, by prioritizing daily obedience and reliance on God. Instead of boasting in religious acts or personal goodness, seek to quietly do what is right and kind in God's eyes. Don't let the deadly sin of pride encourage your own personal agenda, but rather let your faith in the Lord drive you to bring glory to God first and foremost. Even more, let your humility be evident in how you treat others justly and in your dependence on

God in prayer.

Reflection:

Are there areas in your life where outward actions have taken priority over a humble heart? How can you actively practice walking humbly with God today?

* * *

Write your reflections here:

_____

_____

_____

_____

_____

_____

_____

_____

_____

_____

_____

_____

_____

_____

_____

_____

_____

_____

_____

_____

_____

_____

_____

_____

_____

_____

_____

Day 2: Pride Before a Fall

Scripture (NASB95):

Pride goes before destruction, and a haughty spirit before stumbling.

Proverbs 16:18

Insight:

This proverb delivers a sobering warning: an attitude of pride sets the stage for downfall. When we become arrogant or overconfident ("haughty spirit"), we become blind to our vulnerabilities and ignore wise counsel. Eventually, unchecked pride leads to mistakes, failure, or disgrace. The Scripture highlights a universal truth that pride is often the precursor to personal destruction or loss. Trusting in self only leads to failure, but trusting in God makes for wise decisions.

Application:

Guard your heart against arrogance by regularly examining your motives and attitude. If you find yourself thinking "it could never happen to me" or looking down on others, take heed. Cultivate humility through practices such as asking for feedback, admitting mistakes, taking accountability, and remembering past lessons. By staying humble and teachable, you can avoid the stumbling blocks that pride and your ego bring.

Reflection:

Can you recall a time when pride led to an embarrassing or painful situation in your life? What did you learn from it, and how might remembering that lesson keep you humble in the future and aligned with God's will?

* * *

Write your reflections here:

_____
_____
_____
_____
_____
_____
_____
_____
_____
_____
_____
_____
_____
_____
_____
_____
_____
_____
_____
_____
_____
_____
_____
_____
_____
_____
_____
_____
_____
_____

Day 3: Grace to the Humble

Scripture (NASB95):

But He gives a greater grace. Therefore it says, "God is opposed to the proud, but gives grace to the humble."

James 4:6

Insight:

James reminds believers of God's unchanging posture toward pride and humility. Quoting Scripture, he emphasizes that pride actually pits us against God. The proud heart resists God's authority and therefore finds itself resisted by God. In contrast, the humble heart attracts God's favor and help ("greater grace"). Humility, in a biblical sense, means recognizing our need for God, and in response, God generously supplies the grace we need.

Application:

Choose humility as a way of life by acknowledging God in all your ways. Rather than brag about your abilities or rely on your own strength, admit your dependence on Him. When you feel pride creeping up (perhaps in accomplishments or your spiritual life), remember that it distances you from God and His glorious wisdom. Seek His grace through humble prayer and repentance. God promises to pour out grace, wisdom, and strength on those who humbly ask.

Reflection:

In what situations do you sense pride making you resist God's guidance, wisdom, or help? How can you instead submit those areas to God, trusting Him and receiving His "greater grace?"

* * *

Write your reflections here:

_____

_____

_____

_____

_____

_____

_____

_____

_____

_____

_____

_____

_____

_____

_____

_____

_____

_____

_____

_____

_____

_____

_____

_____

_____

_____

_____

_____

_____

Day 4: Exalted Through Humility

Scripture (NASB95):

"For everyone who exalts himself will be humbled, and he who humbles himself will be exalted."

Luke 14:11

Insight:

Here, Jesus teaches a kingdom principle often repeated in Scripture, such as Luke 18:14, Matthew 18:4, and Matthew 23:12. In the context of a parable about seeking the lowest seat at a banquet, He explains that God will ultimately reverse the fortunes of the proud and the humble. Those who push themselves upward in self-promotion will be brought low by God, whereas those who voluntarily take a humble position will, in due time, be honored by God at the final judgment. This "great reversal" shows that true honor in God's eyes comes through humility, not self-exaltation.

Application:

Practice taking the "lower seat" in your daily life. This could mean letting others go first, giving credit to teammates instead of seeking recognition for yourself, or serving on tasks without seeking personal gain. Trust that promotion and honor are in God's hands, not yours. When you feel tempted to boast or assert your importance, remember Jesus' words and choose the humble path—regardless of the situation. In doing so, you leave room for God to lift you up at the proper time.

Reflection:

Are you seeking recognition or status in any area of your life? What would it look like to humble yourself in that situation and let God handle any exaltation or credit that might come? How might you overcome the emotional feelings associated with the desire for recognition or status?

* * *

Write your reflections here:

_____
_____
_____
_____
_____
_____
_____
_____
_____
_____
_____
_____
_____
_____
_____
_____
_____
_____
_____
_____
_____
_____
_____
_____
_____
_____
_____
_____
_____
_____
_____

Day 5: Humility in Self-Assessment

Scripture (NASB95):

For through the grace given to me I say to everyone among you not to think more highly of himself than he ought to think, but to think so as to have sound judgment.

Romans 12:3

Insight:

The Apostle Paul urges believers to adopt a humble and realistic view of themselves. We are warned against an inflated self-opinion ("more highly... than he ought") and encouraged instead toward "sound judgment" – an honest, sober appraisal of our own strengths and weaknesses. This kind of humility doesn't mean belittling ourselves; it means recognizing that any gifts or abilities we have are from God ("through the grace given to me") and that we all have limitations. There is no room for prideful and inflated egos among Christ followers.

Application:

Practice honest self-assessment by regularly inviting God (and even trusted friends) to show you areas of pride in your life. A practical step is to celebrate others' gifts and accept your own limitations. For example, instead of thinking you're the only one who is right or capable, acknowledge the contributions and wisdom of others. When you succeed, give glory to God and remember that you still have room to grow (as we all do and will continue to do). When you fail, be honest about it and learn from the encounter rather than protecting your ego.

Reflection:

Do you secretly view yourself as superior to others in intelligence, spirituality, or ability? How can you cultivate a more honest and humble self-image that aligns with "sound judgment?" That is, neither puffed up with pride nor falsely modest.

* * *

Write your reflections here:

_____

_____

_____

_____

_____

_____

_____

_____

_____

_____

_____

_____

_____

_____

_____

_____

_____

_____

_____

_____

_____

_____

_____

_____

_____

_____

_____

_____

Day 6: Christ's Example of Humility

Scripture (NASB95):

Have this attitude in yourselves which was also in Christ Jesus, who, although He existed in the form of God, did not regard equality with God a thing to be grasped, but emptied Himself, taking the form of a bond-servant, and being made in the likeness of men. Being found in appearance as a man, He humbled Himself by becoming obedient to the point of death, even death on a cross.

Philippians 2:5–8

Insight:

Jesus Christ is our ultimate model of humility. Though He is God, He laid aside His divine privileges ("emptied Himself") to become human and live as a servant. His humility is seen in the Incarnation (taking on flesh) and in His obedience to the Father's will all the way to dying on the cross like a criminal. This profound passage teaches that humility involves self-emptying and obedience. Jesus didn't cling to His rights or status; instead, He voluntarily lowered Himself for the sake of others. We are called to adopt this same attitude, the self-giving of Christ, in our relationships and lives.

* * *

Application:

Follow Christ's example by letting go of selfish ambition and entitlement. Ask, "How can I serve others and obey God's will today, even at personal cost?" Perhaps it means giving up a convenience or honor you deserve, or feel you deserve, to help someone in need. Maybe it's forgiving an offense or attack against you, or doing a task no one else wants to do. Remember, no act of humility you do could ever be as great as the massive step down that Jesus did for you, but you can serve and sacrifice with gratitude that you are walking in our Master's footsteps.

Reflection:

What would it look like for you to "empty yourself" of status or privilege in a specific situation right now? How can Christ's immense humility, leaving heaven and embracing the Cross, inspire you to act on a humble, servant's mindset toward the people in your life?

* * *

Write your reflections here:

_____
_____
_____
_____
_____
_____
_____
_____
_____
_____
_____
_____
_____
_____
_____
_____
_____
_____
_____
_____
_____
_____
_____
_____
_____
_____
_____
_____
_____

Day 7: Humility in Service

Scripture (NASB95):

"If I then, the Lord and the Teacher, washed your feet, you also ought to wash one another's feet. For I gave you an example that you also should do as I did to you."

John 13:14–15

Insight:

On the night of the Last Supper, Jesus performed one of the lowliest tasks imaginable in His culture: washing His disciples' feet. In this passage, after finishing, He explains the lesson. Despite being their Master and Teacher, Jesus humbled Himself to serve, reversing the world's idea of leadership. He then charges His followers to imitate His example by serving each other in humble, practical ways. True greatness in Christ's eyes is expressed through servanthood, not position. And humility ultimately brings exaltation.

Application:

Look for opportunities to "wash feet" in your context. In modern terms, this means doing humble tasks that benefit others without concern for your dignity or reward. It could be cleaning up after others, caring for someone who can't return the favor, or simply putting others' needs first in everyday routines. Let Christ's example challenge any attitude that says, "That job is beneath me." Instead, willingly take on acts of service, knowing that when you serve the least, you are following Jesus' example of authentic leadership.

Reflection:

How do you react to lowly tasks or invisible service? Identify one humble act of service you can do this week (perhaps something no one else wants to do). How might performing that service with a willing heart help cultivate Christ-like humility in you?

* * *

Write your reflections here:

_____

_____

_____

_____

_____

_____

_____

_____

_____

_____

_____

_____

_____

_____

_____

_____

_____

_____

_____

_____

_____

_____

_____

_____

_____

_____

_____

_____

_____

Day 8: Gentle and Humble in Heart

Scripture (NASB95):

"Take My yoke upon you and learn from Me, for I am gentle and humble in heart, and you will find rest for your souls."

Matthew 11:29

Insight:

In this gracious invitation, Jesus reveals His own heart and character. He describes Himself as "gentle and humble in heart." Unlike the heavy burdens placed by proud religious leaders of His day, Jesus offers a "yoke" (His teaching and lordship) that is kind and life-giving. To learn from Jesus means to adopt His gentle, lowly heart attitude and be obedient, subordinate, and servant-oriented. Remarkably, He ties our finding *rest* for our souls to accepting His humble way. Pride leads to restlessness and stress, but Christ-like humility leads to peace and relief because we stop trying to prove ourselves and instead trust in Him.

Application:

Come to Jesus with your burdens and practice learning from His humility. This could mean relinquishing the pride that says, "I must handle it all myself." Instead, submit to His guidance ("take My yoke"). In interactions, strive to be gentle and meek, as Jesus is.

For example, respond softly when provoked or be patient with someone who is struggling. As you do, you will experience more of the inner rest that Jesus promises, because humility frees you from the noisy struggle of self-importance and ego-driven responses.

Reflection:

In what areas of life are you feeling weary or burdened? How might embracing Jesus' gentle and humble way (for instance, asking Him for help or responding to challenges with meekness) bring rest to your weary and burdened soul?

* * *

Write your reflections here:

_____
_____
_____
_____
_____
_____
_____
_____
_____
_____
_____
_____
_____
_____
_____
_____
_____
_____
_____
_____
_____
_____
_____
_____
_____
_____
_____
_____

Day 9: Considering Others First

Scripture (NASB95):

Do nothing from selfishness or empty conceit, but with humility of mind regard one another as more important than yourselves; do not merely look out for your own personal interests, but also for the interests of others.

Philippians 2:3–4

Insight:

These verses instruct us on the practical outworking of humility in community. We're called to reject selfish ambition and vanity ("empty conceit") and instead adopt an others-centered mindset. "Humility of mind" here means a lowliness of mind that frees us to value others highly. It doesn't mean thinking poorly of ourselves or not being mindful of our own affairs; it means focusing less on self altogether. Verse 4 clarifies that humility leads us to pay attention to others' needs, not just our own. This attitude mirrors Christ's mindset and fosters unity and love among believers.

Application:

Make a conscious effort to put this into practice by esteeming and serving those around you. For example, in a conversation, listen more than you talk about yourself. Don't listen to respond; instead, consciously listen and empathize or engage with the other person's conversation. In family or work decisions, consider others' needs and preferences before insisting on your way. You might volunteer to help someone reach their goal even if it doesn't benefit you. Such actions cultivate a humble heart and strengthen relationships. Remember, regarding others as "more important" doesn't mean you think poorly of yourself; it means you choose to elevate others in how you treat them.

Reflection:

In your daily routines, whose interests have you been overlooking due to self-focus? What is one specific way you can consider the needs or preferences of that person (or group) and take action to serve or honor them this week?

* * *

Write your reflections here:

_____

_____

_____

_____

_____

_____

_____

_____

_____

_____

_____

_____

_____

_____

_____

_____

_____

_____

_____

_____

_____

_____

_____

_____

_____

_____

_____

_____

Day 10: Clothe Yourself with Humility

Scripture (NASB95):

All of you, clothe yourselves with humility toward one another, for "God is opposed to the proud, but gives grace to the humble." Humble yourselves, therefore, under the mighty hand of God, that He may exalt you at the proper time.

1 Peter 5:5–6

Insight:

Peter addresses the entire church ("all of you"), using the vivid metaphor of putting on, or girding, yourself in clothing. Just as we intentionally dress ourselves each day, we are to adopt deliberately, or gird, humility in how we relate to one another. Peter reinforces why: pride sets us against God (echoing James 4:6 and Proverbs 3:34) and puts God's flock (His people) in peril, whereas humility invites His grace, love, and protection. Furthermore, verse 6 assures us that if we humble ourselves under God's authority, He will lift us up at the right time. This could mean receiving honor, opportunity, or relief according to His perfect timing.

Application:

"Get dressed" in humility each morning by praying for

a servant's heart before you interact with others. Practically, clothing yourself in humility might look like being quick to apologize or to defer credit. But it also means submitting to God's leadership, trusting Him when you feel you're in a low place, and resisting the urge to force your own promotion. Instead of striving in pride, faithfully do what God asks and leave the results to Him. Remember that God sees and, in due season, will exalt the humble.

Reflection:

What would it mean for you to "wear" or "gird" humility in your current season of life (at home, work, church)? Are you willing to let go of self-promotion and trust that God's "mighty hand" is working for your good and others' in His timing?

* * *

Write your reflections here:

_____
_____
_____
_____
_____
_____
_____
_____
_____
_____
_____
_____
_____
_____
_____
_____
_____
_____
_____
_____
_____
_____
_____
_____
_____
_____
_____
_____

Day 11: Avoid Self-Praise

Scripture (NASB95):

Let another praise you, and not your own mouth; a stranger, and not your own lips.

Proverbs 27:2

Insight:

This proverb offers wise counsel about how we handle recognition. It pointedly tells us to refrain from praising ourselves. Boasting about our accomplishments or qualities is a form of pride that is both unbecoming and unreliable. The verse suggests that if praise is due, it ought to come from someone else's lips. In other words, our actions should speak for themselves, and we should resist the urge to trumpet our own praise. Humility is content to work hard quietly and allow any recognition to come naturally from others (if at all), rather than from self-promotion.

Application:

In practice, this means biting your tongue on occasions when you want to make sure others know about your successes or virtues. Instead of steering conversations to highlight your achievements, practice highlighting others' strengths. If you receive a compliment, say "thank you" rather than one-upping it or fishing for more. You can also ask God to purify your motives by

His wisdom, so that you serve and do good without needing applause. By letting others do the praising (or not), you grow in the freedom and grace of humility.

Reflection:

Pay attention to your speech: do you tend to announce your own accomplishments or qualities? Next time you feel the impulse to praise yourself (even subtly), how could you respond differently in line with this proverb? If you recall a time in which you announced your own accomplishments or qualities, how did others react, and how did the situation unfold?

* * *

Write your reflections here:

Day 12: Humility in Community

Scripture (NASB95):

Be of the same mind toward one another; do not be haughty in mind, but associate with the lowly. Do not be wise in your own estimation.

Romans 12:16

Insight:

Paul continues his exhortations on Christian living by addressing our mindset in the community of faith. "Being of the same mind" suggests living in harmony and treating each other as equals. To do this, we must "not be haughty." In other words, we should not consider ourselves too high-ranking to spend time with people of humble position or circumstances. He urges believers to willingly associate with those who are "lowly" (the poor, the socially unimpressive, or anyone the world might deem insignificant). The final admonition, "do not be wise in your own estimation," reinforces the call to abandon conceit. Thinking we are constantly right or above others destroys unity; humility in Christ builds it and expands our mercy and love.

Application:

Seek out opportunities to connect with and learn from people who might otherwise be overlooked. For example, at church or social gatherings, make an effort to converse with someone new or someone who might be marginalized, rather than gravitating only to those who seem influential or who boost your ego. Consciously reject thoughts of elitism, whether based on education, wealth, or background. When conflicts or differences of opinion arise, remind yourself not to assume you're the only one with wisdom; instead, listen respectfully to others. As you practice these things, you create an atmosphere and culture where everyone is valued, and unity can flourish.

Reflection:

Do you tend to gravitate towards people who are like you or whom you consider impressive? How can you break out of that comfort zone and show Christ-like love to someone whom others might overlook? Additionally, in disagreements, what would it look like to not be "wise in your own sight" but to remain open and humble?

* * *

Write your reflections here:

_____
_____
_____
_____
_____
_____
_____
_____
_____
_____
_____
_____
_____
_____
_____
_____
_____
_____
_____
_____
_____
_____
_____
_____
_____
_____
_____
_____
_____

Day 13: Humility in Prayer

Scripture (NASB95):

"But the tax collector, standing some distance away, was even unwilling to lift up his eyes to heaven, but was beating his breast, saying, 'God, be merciful to me, the sinner!' I tell you, this man went to his house justified rather than the other; for everyone who exalts himself will be humbled, but he who humbles himself will be exalted."

Luke 18:13–14

Insight:

Jesus spoke this parable to expose the danger of self-righteous pride in our approach to God. The tax collector's posture and words show genuine humility: he stood afar, wouldn't even lift his eyes, and pleaded for and requested mercy as a sinner. In stark contrast, the Pharisee (not quoted here, but in verses 11–12) had prayed, boasting of his righteousness. Jesus declares that it was the humble, repentant tax collector, not the proud religious man, who left justified (forgiven and right with God). God responds to a contrite heart, and no amount of spiritual résumé can replace humble repentance. The concluding principle repeats: self-exaltation leads to humbling, but self-humbling leads to exaltation (in this context, the exaltation is being forgiven and accepted by God).

Application:

When you pray, come as the tax collector did—aware of your need for mercy rather than listing your merits. Regularly confess your sins and weaknesses to God instead of approaching Him as if you've earned favor. In practical terms, this might involve kneeling or bowing your head, not as a ritual, but as a genuine expression of reverence. It also means rejecting any attitude that looks down on others' spiritual state; focus on your own heart before God. By cultivating a humble prayer life, you keep your relationship with God authentic and grace-filled.

Reflection:

Consider your recent prayers: do they resemble the Pharisee's (self-congratulatory) or the tax collector's (humble and penitent)? How can you foster a more humble posture in prayer, both inwardly (attitude) and outwardly (perhaps by literally kneeling or using words of dependence)?

* * *

Write your reflections here:

Day 14: Childlike Humility

Scripture (NASB95):

"Whoever then humbles himself as this child, he is the greatest in the kingdom of heaven."

Matthew 18:4

Insight:

The disciples had been arguing about who was the greatest in God's kingdom, and Jesus responded by placing a little child in their midst (Matthew 18:1–3 for context). He points to the child's lowly status and trusting nature as a model. In that society, children had no power or prestige; they depended on others. Jesus teaches that true greatness in His kingdom comes from humbling oneself like a child, letting go of claims to status, and embracing dependence and trust. It's a radical redefinition of greatness: humility and simplicity, not power or pride, mark the "greatest" in God's eyes. Entering the kingdom of God requires walking humbly, not arrogantly.

Application:

Embrace a childlike attitude in your faith and daily life. This means trusting God the way a little child trusts a loving father with simplicity and sincerity. In practice, you can cultivate childlike humility by being quick to forgive, eager to learn, and free of pretension. Children don't worry about titles or accolades; they live in the moment and depend on their parents. Likewise, try releasing your grip on the desire for recognition or control, and choose to be content with obscurity if that's where God has you. Remember, your value comes from God's love, not from asserting yourself over others.

Reflection:

In what ways do you find it difficult to "become like a child"? (For instance, admitting you need help, not overcomplicating your faith, or relinquishing status.) What is one practical step you can take to cultivate childlike humility and trust in your relationship with God and others?

* * *

Write your reflections here:

_____

_____

_____

_____

_____

_____

_____

_____

_____

_____

_____

_____

_____

_____

_____

_____

_____

_____

_____

_____

_____

_____

_____

_____

_____

_____

Day 15: Humbled by God

Scripture (NASB95):

Now I, Nebuchadnezzar, praise, exalt, and honor the King of heaven, for all His works are true and His ways just; and He is able to humble those who walk in pride.

Daniel 4:37

Insight:

These are the closing words of King Nebuchadnezzar's astonishing personal testimony. Nebuchadnezzar was a powerful Babylonian king who had exalted himself and taken credit for his glorious kingdom (Daniel 4:30). In response, God struck him with a period of insanity, where the king lived like an animal, until he acknowledged God's sovereignty. Once his sanity and kingdom were restored, Nebuchadnezzar publicly confessed this truth: God is supreme, and He can humble anyone who lives in pride. The proud king learned the hard way that all he had was from God, and God alone deserves the highest honor.

Application:

Take Nebuchadnezzar's hard-learned lesson to heart: if you find yourself "walking in pride," whether in success, leadership, or personal achievements, remember that God can take it all away in a moment. Rather than forcing God to oppose your pride, willingly humble yourself. Acknowledge God as the source of every blessing and ability you have. One practical way is through thanksgiving by regularly praising and thanking the "King of heaven" for your accomplishments, giving Him credit instead of yourself. By doing so, you honor God's sovereignty and potentially spare yourself from a humbling ordeal.

Reflection:

Nebuchadnezzar declared that God can humble the proud. Do you see any prideful attitudes in your life that, if left unchecked, might invite God's humbling hand? How can you proactively humble yourself now (through repentance, gratitude, or giving God glory) in those areas? Also, have you ever experienced God humbling your pride? How did you respond and change your behavior?

* * *

Write your reflections here:

_____

_____

_____

_____

_____

_____

_____

_____

_____

_____

_____

_____

_____

_____

_____

_____

_____

_____

_____

_____

_____

_____

_____

_____

_____

_____

_____

_____

_____

_____

_____

Day 16: Pride Brings Dishonor

Scripture (NASB95):

When pride comes, then comes dishonor, but with the humble is wisdom.

Proverbs 11:2

Insight:

This proverb teaches a cause-and-effect principle observed in life. Pride ultimately leads to disgrace or shame ("dishonor"). A prideful person may elevate themselves for a time, but it often ends in a fall that brings embarrassment. We can think of biblical examples like Haman in the Book of Esther: in his pride, he planned to honor himself and destroy a humble man (Mordecai), but instead, Haman was humiliated and defeated. On the flip side, the second half of the verse tells us that humility accompanies wisdom and integrity. A humble heart is teachable and fears the Lord, which is the beginning of both wisdom and integrity. Thus, humility tends to bring honor and respect in the long run (as God blesses the humble).

Application:

Take this wisdom to heart by actively resisting the temptation to boast or act arrogantly. If you achieve something great, receive any compliments graciously, but refrain from self-glorification. Remember that pride makes us blind to our mistakes, while humility keeps us open to advice and correction. Cultivate humility by seeking wisdom from others (mentors, scripture, feedback). For example, if you're in a conflict, humble yourself enough to consider the other person's perspective or admit where you might be wrong. In doing so, you'll avoid the shame that pride brings and walk in the honor and good sense that humility affords.

Reflection:

Think of a situation (past or present) where your pride might lead, or has led, to embarrassment or conflict. How could embracing humility and wisdom in that situation change the outcome? What is one step you can take to replace pride with humility this week?

* * *

Write your reflections here:

_____

_____

_____

_____

_____

_____

_____

_____

_____

_____

_____

_____

_____

_____

_____

_____

_____

_____

_____

_____

_____

_____

_____

_____

_____

_____

_____

_____

Day 17: The Perils of Pride

Scripture (NASB95):

But when he became strong, his heart was so proud that he acted corruptly and he was unfaithful to the LORD his God.

2 Chronicles 26:16

Insight:

This verse describes King Uzziah of Judah at the height of his success. Uzziah started as a godly king, and God helped him become powerful and famous. However, as his power grew, so did his pride. "When he became strong, his heart was lifted up," and that pride led him into sin. Specifically, Uzziah arrogantly violated God's command by entering the temple to burn incense, a duty only for priests. God struck him with leprosy as punishment (see 2 Chronicles 26:17–21). Uzziah's story illustrates how success can breed pride, which then leads to downfall and unfaithfulness. No matter how "strong" we become, we never outgrow our need for humble obedience to God.

Application:

If God has given you success, whether in career, ministry, or personal growth, stay on guard. Pride can creep in subtly with each achievement. Combat this by continually giving God credit and by maintaining accountability. Welcome the counsel or even rebuke of trusted friends as a safeguard against corrupt decisions. Remember that spiritual faithfulness matters more than worldly success. For instance, if you find yourself cutting ethical corners or neglecting prayer because you feel self-sufficient, recognize that as pride. Return to dependence on God through practices like regular prayer, worship, and remembering His past mercies. Let Uzziah's example be a warning: never let your strength make you forget your Source, or a humiliated stain could be your future.

Reflection:

How do you respond inwardly when you experience success or praise? Do you, like Uzziah, feel your heart "lift up" with self-importance? Identify one habit that can keep you grounded (such as journaling gratitude to God or inviting a mentor to speak into your life) and commit to it, especially in seasons of prosperity.

* * *

Write your reflections here:

_____

_____

_____

_____

_____

_____

_____

_____

_____

_____

_____

_____

_____

_____

_____

_____

_____

_____

_____

_____

_____

_____

_____

_____

_____

_____

_____

_____

Day 18: Stealing God's Glory

Scripture (NASB95):

The people kept crying out, "The voice of a god and not of a man!" And immediately an angel of the Lord struck him because he did not give God the glory, and he was eaten by worms and died.

Acts 12:22–23

Insight:

This startling event concerns Herod Agrippa I, a king who persecuted the early church. On one occasion, Herod donned his royal apparel and addressed a crowd. Enamored by his presence, the people shouted that his voice was that of a god. Herod accepted this blasphemous flattery instead of redirecting honor to God. The result was immediate and sobering: God struck Herod down for his pride and sacrilege. The mention of being "eaten by worms" underscores the disgrace and divine judgment he faced. This account powerfully demonstrates God's intolerance for humans who try to usurp His glory. It's a New Testament echo of the principle that God opposes the proud and, conversely, vindicates His holiness.

Application:

While our situations may not be as dramatic, we should be careful to *give God the glory* in our lives. This means that if you receive praise or achieve something noteworthy, acknowledge God's hand in it, both internally and externally. For instance, you might say, "I'm thankful to God for this accomplishment," or quietly pray a prayer of thanks when complimented. Additionally, be wary of craving praise that belongs to God—such as spiritual pride that wants credit for ministry impact or moral standing. Deflect that glory upward. Remember that any talents, opportunities, or victories you have ultimately come from the Lord. By cultivating gratitude and redirecting praise, you walk in humility and avoid the subtle trap of "playing god" in your own story.

Reflection:

Consider moments when others praise you: do you secretly revel in it as Herod did, or do you consciously attribute the credit to God? How might you practice giving God glory in your daily successes and talents? Try to identify one area where you can more openly or intentionally honor God's role in your achievements.

* * *

Write your reflections here:

_____
_____
_____
_____
_____
_____
_____
_____
_____
_____
_____
_____
_____
_____
_____
_____
_____
_____
_____
_____
_____
_____
_____
_____
_____
_____
_____
_____
_____
_____

Day 19: I Must Decrease

Scripture (NASB95):

"He must increase, but I must decrease."

John 3:30

Insight:

These famous words were spoken by John the Baptist when his followers were concerned that people were flocking to Jesus rather than John. John understood his God-given role as the forerunner to Christ. In this simple, profound statement, he joyfully expresses his hope that his own influence will wane as Jesus' grows. He did not turn to jealousy but rather joy. John's humility is evident, and he likens himself to the "friend of the bridegroom" who rejoices at the bridegroom's voice (John 3:29). This attitude teaches us that our lives as believers are meant to point to Christ, not to ourselves. True humility in ministry or any endeavor for God is desiring Christ's fame above our own.

Application:

Adopt John's motto in your daily life and seek ways to make Jesus more visible and yourself less. Practically, this could mean sharing testimonies of what Christ has done (instead of what *you* have done). In your workplace or church service, work not for personal recognition, but so that Christ's character is displayed through you. If you have a platform or leadership position, use it to spotlight Jesus and serve others, not to build your brand. It may also mean happily stepping aside when someone else can do a job better or when God is moving you in a new direction. Find joy, as John did, in Jesus being exalted, even if it means your personal spotlight dims.

Reflection:

Can you echo John's heart by honestly saying you want Jesus to increase in every aspect of your life? What would "decreasing" look like for you personally (perhaps in how you handle credit, leadership, or ambition)? Pray about one specific area where you can step back and let Christ take center stage.

***

Write your reflections here:

_____
_____
_____
_____
_____
_____
_____
_____
_____
_____
_____
_____
_____
_____
_____
_____
_____
_____
_____
_____
_____
_____
_____
_____
_____
_____
_____
_____
_____

Day 20: The Meekest Man

Scripture (NASB95):

Now the man Moses was very humble, more than any man who was on the face of the earth.

Numbers 12:3

Insight:

This parenthetical comment in Scripture speaks volumes about Moses' character. Moses had an extraordinary calling and walked closely with God, yet he is noted for his exceedingly humble (or "meek") character. The context of Numbers 12 is telling: Moses' siblings, Aaron and Miriam, were criticizing him, and Moses did not defend himself. Instead, God defended Moses, even inflicting leprosy on Miriam for her prideful challenge. Moses, in turn, interceded for her healing. Moses' humility was demonstrated in his patience, his reliance on God to vindicate him, and his forgiving, servant's heart. True meekness, as Moses exemplified, is power under control. He had great authority but did not wield it for ego.

Application:

Learning from Moses, aim to respond to criticism or provocation with meekness rather than defensiveness. When you feel misunderstood or attacked, pause and pray rather than immediately asserting your rights.

Trust that if you are in the right, God can vindicate you. Additionally, use any leadership or influence you have to serve others gently. Moses often fell on his face to pray for the very people who challenged him. Consider how you might pray for or bless those who oppose you. Cultivating meekness may involve biting your tongue, letting someone else get the last word, or extending kindness when you could enforce authority. Remember, meekness is not weakness; it's strength and devout dependence submitted to God's control.

Reflection:

How do you react when you're challenged or criticized? Do you rush to defend your honor, or are you willing to stay quiet and let God handle it? Identify one situation in your life where you can practice "the meekness of Moses" (perhaps by listening more, refraining from retaliation, or praying for someone who has mistreated you).

* * *

Write your reflections here:

_____
_____
_____
_____
_____
_____
_____
_____
_____
_____
_____
_____
_____
_____
_____
_____
_____
_____
_____
_____
_____
_____
_____
_____
_____
_____
_____
_____
_____

Day 21: God Lifts Up the Humble

Scripture (NASB95):

He has done mighty deeds with His arm; He has scattered those who were proud in the thoughts of their heart. He has brought down rulers from their thrones, and has exalted those who were humble.

Luke 1:51–52

Insight:

These lines come from Mary's Magnificat (Luke 1:46–55), a song of praise she offered to God during her pregnancy with Jesus. In it, Mary marvels at how God overturns human expectations: He shows strength by scattering the proud and dethroning rulers, and He exalts the humble. Mary herself was a lowly young woman of no social status, yet God chose her to bear the Messiah. Her song recognizes a consistent biblical theme that God actively opposes pride and lifts up the humble (both spiritually and, at times, in tangible ways). This doesn't always happen on our timetable, but ultimately God will right wrongs and reward the lowly who trust in Him.

Application:

Take comfort and hope in God's heart for the humble. If you're in a humble or unfair circumstance, know that God sees you and, in His time, can turn things around.

Continue to walk in humility even when it seems like the proud prosper. On a practical level, this might mean faithfully doing good without immediate recognition, trusting that God notices. It could also mean refusing to adopt cutthroat, prideful tactics to advance yourself and believing that promotion comes from the Lord. Rejoice with those of low position and empathize with the oppressed, knowing God often works through the "least." Like Mary, make praise your response and thank God that He values and raises up the humble.

Reflection:

Where do you see examples of this significant reversal in your own life or community (the humble lifted up, the proud brought low)? How can you align with God's way by esteeming humility over power? If you feel "lowly" right now, how does Mary's song encourage you to remain faithful and humble?

* * *

Write your reflections here:

_____
_____
_____
_____
_____
_____
_____
_____
_____
_____
_____
_____
_____
_____
_____
_____
_____
_____
_____
_____
_____
_____
_____
_____
_____
_____
_____

Day 22: Strength in Weakness

Scripture (NASB95):

And He has said to me, "My grace is sufficient for you, for power is perfected in weakness." Most gladly, therefore, I will rather boast about my weaknesses, so that the power of Christ may dwell in me. ... For when I am weak, then I am strong.

2 Corinthians 12:9–10

Insight:

The Apostle Paul shares a counterintuitive revelation he received from the Lord. After praying for a "thorn in the flesh" to be removed, he got this answer: God's grace is enough, and His power is made perfect in our weakness. Instead of removing the difficulty, God would show His strength through Paul's humility and dependence. Paul's response is remarkable; he actually chooses to boast in his weaknesses! But why? Because those weaknesses became the very platform for Christ's power. In recognizing his own frailty, Paul created room for God's strength to work, turning human weakness into an opportunity for divine strength. This teaches us a form of humility where we can accept and even glory in our limitations because they showcase God's greatness.

* * *

Application:

Embrace your own weaknesses and struggles as places for God to work, rather than hiding or being ashamed of them. In practice, this could mean being honest with others about where you need prayer or help, rather than maintaining a proud front of self-sufficiency. It means when you face a trial that you feel inadequate to handle, instead of despairing or pretending to have it all together, you lean into God's grace through prayer and perhaps counsel from others. Try reframing a current weakness. Instead of saying "I can't do this, it's a liability," say "This is where I especially need Christ's strength." Boasting in weakness isn't complaining; it's testifying that any strength or victory you have comes from God.

Reflection:

What is a "thorn" or weakness in your life that you've been despising or hiding? How might you approach it differently if you believed God's power works best when you know you need Him? Consider sharing this area with a trusted friend or mentor and invite Christ's power to shine through your admitted weakness.

* * *

Write your reflections here:

_____
_____
_____
_____
_____
_____
_____
_____
_____
_____
_____
_____
_____
_____
_____
_____
_____
_____
_____
_____
_____
_____
_____
_____
_____
_____
_____
_____
_____
_____
_____

Day 23: Love Is Not Proud

Scripture (NASB95):

Love is patient, love is kind and is not jealous; love does not brag and is not arrogant.

1 Corinthians 13:4

Insight:

In the famous "Love Chapter," Paul describes the characteristics of true *agape* love. Notably, two of those descriptors deal directly with pride: love doesn't boast (no bragging) and isn't arrogant (no inflated ego). This teaches us that there is no room for selfish pride in genuine love. If we are acting pridefully, seeking to show off, feeling superior, or insisting on our own way, we are not acting in love. Love, by nature, focuses on the beloved rather than the self. It's humble, willing to take a lower place for the good of another. By contrast, pride puts self at the center. Thus, to genuinely love others (as Christ calls us to), we must renounce prideful attitudes and actions.

Application:

Evaluate your relationships through the lens of 1 Corinthians 13: Are you exhibiting a love that's free of bragging and arrogance? In practice, you can work on this by choosing to listen to and value others' stories instead of steering conversations back to yourself.

Refrain from one-upping someone's experience with your own. In disagreements with a loved one, instead of letting pride make you defensive, try to empathize and even admit fault if applicable. Serve in small ways that no one sees, as this trains your heart to love without needing applause. By deliberately practicing humility in your daily interactions (like apologizing first, or letting someone else receive credit), you align with the loving character of Christ.

Reflection:

How do pride and self-interest sometimes taint the way you treat those you care about? For instance, do you find yourself needing to be "right" or praised in your family, friendships, or marriage? Identify one prideful habit that harms your ability to love (such as interrupting, correcting often, or bragging), and plan a concrete change to practice humble love instead.

* * *

Write your reflections here:

_____
_____
_____
_____
_____
_____
_____
_____
_____
_____
_____
_____
_____
_____
_____
_____
_____
_____
_____
_____
_____
_____
_____
_____
_____
_____

Day 24: The Pride of Life

Scripture (NASB95):

For all that is in the world, the lust of the flesh and the lust of the eyes and the boastful pride of life, is not from the Father, but is from the world.

1 John 2:16

Insight:

The "pride of life" refers to the arrogant confidence in one's own resources, abilities, or status. Essentially, worldly pride in what one has and does. The Apostle John warns that this, along with fleshly lusts and greed ("lust of eyes"), characterizes the fallen world's values, not God's. The pride of life might manifest as a craving for recognition, a drive to impress others, or an attitude of self-sufficiency that excludes God. John starkly states that such pride doesn't come from the Father. In fact, in the next verse (1 John 2:17), he reminds us that the world and its lusts are passing away. Investing our identity in earthly achievements or possessions is both sinful and ultimately futile.

Application:

Take inventory of what you're most proud of in life (education, career, looks, possessions, social media image, etc.). While there's nothing wrong with enjoying God's gifts or celebrating hard work, guard against making them your identity or a source of boasting. Practice the opposite of the world's pride by cultivating gratitude and contentment. For example, when you receive a promotion or buy something nice, thank God and keep it in perspective rather than flaunting it. Simplify when you can; it trains the soul to rely on God, not stuff. Also, intentionally give God credit in conversations for any "life achievements" you share about. Remember, the secure foundation is doing God's will (1 John 2:17), not chasing status.

Reflection:

In what ways are you tempted by the "pride of life"? Do you find yourself showing off accomplishments or feeling superior because of what you have or know? How can you redirect those temptations into opportunities to glorify God and serve others? Consider one practical step, such as privately helping someone who can't repay you or refraining from posting a braggy update, to break the habit of worldly pride.

* * *

Write your reflections here:

_____
_____
_____
_____
_____
_____
_____
_____
_____
_____
_____
_____
_____
_____
_____
_____
_____
_____
_____
_____
_____
_____
_____
_____
_____
_____
_____

Day 25: Humility in Planning – "If the Lord Wills"

Scripture (NASB95):

Instead, you ought to say, "If the Lord wills, we will live and also do this or that." But as it is, you boast in your arrogance; all such boasting is evil.

James 4:15–16

Insight:

James addresses believers who made confident plans about the future without acknowledging God. He isn't discouraging planning itself, but rather the presumptuous attitude behind statements like "Tomorrow we will go to this city, spend a year there, and make a profit" (see James 4:13). Such speech, James says, is boasting about our own control over life; a control we don't truly have. The antidote is to remember our dependence on God's will for every breath and endeavor: "If the Lord wills, we will live and do this or that." Saying "Lord willing" is more than a phrase; it's a mindset of humility that recognizes God's sovereignty over our lives. Boasting as if we are sovereign is not just foolish. James calls it evil because it edges God out of the picture.

* * *

Application:

Cultivate a humble heart about the future. When you make plans (big life plans or even daily schedules), do so prayerfully, asking God to guide and ultimately accomplish His will. Get into the habit of mentally (or verbally) adding "Lord willing" to your intentions. For instance, "We plan to move next year; Lord willing," or "I'll see you tomorrow; if God allows." This isn't superstition; it's a reminder to yourself and others that God is in control. Additionally, hold your plans loosely. If things don't go as you hoped, instead of reacting in frustration or panic, practice surrender. Trust that God may have redirected stuff for a reason. Planning with humility means being flexible and teachable when God's Providence changes your course.

Reflection:

Think about your short-term and long-term plans. Have you invited God into them, truly yielding them to His will? How do you respond when your plans fall apart or get interrupted? Ask God to reveal any arrogance in how you approach your future, and consider starting times of planning or goal-setting with a prayer like, "Lord, what do *You* will in this?"

* * *

Write your reflections here:

_____
_____
_____
_____
_____
_____
_____
_____
_____
_____
_____
_____
_____
_____
_____
_____
_____
_____
_____
_____
_____
_____
_____
_____
_____
_____
_____
_____
_____
_____

Day 26: Blessed are the Meek

Scripture (NASB95):

"Blessed are the gentle (meek), for they shall inherit the earth."

Matthew 5:5

Insight:

In the Beatitudes, Jesus pronounces blessedness on qualities the world often overlooks. "Gentle" here is frequently translated as "meek," meaning a humble, mild disposition. Far from being weak, meekness is power under restraint and an attitude of patience and contentment with God's control. Jesus promises that the meek "shall inherit the earth," echoing Psalm 37:11. Ultimately, in God's kingdom, those who humbly trust in God will receive the inheritance of reigning with Christ (in the renewed earth to come). Even now, the meek are "blessed" because they live free from the turmoil of pride and aggression. This beatitude flips worldly wisdom. It's not the pushy or self-important who are truly happy and destined for reward, but the quietly faithful and humble.

Application:

Strive to be gentle and meek in your interactions. Meekness can be demonstrated by how you handle conflict. Instead of forcing your way, respond softly and yield when appropriate. It also shows in contentment; the meek person isn't constantly grasping for more or envying others, but trusts God's provision. Try practicing meekness by letting someone else take the lead or credit, even if you could assert yourself. Another aspect is patiently enduring provocation without lashing back, trusting that God sees and will set things right. Memorize this beatitude and recall it when you feel pressure to adopt the world's aggressive tactics. Jesus assures you that meekness is not a loss; it's a gain, ultimately leading to an eternal inheritance that far outweighs temporary power plays.

Reflection:

Do you believe that "the meek" are truly blessed and will inherit what's best? Where do you feel tension between Jesus' promise and the world's way of doing things (for example, at work or in personal ambitions)? Identify one scenario where you can consciously choose gentleness or humility over force or pride, and observe how it affects your peace and the outcome.

* * *

Write your reflections here:

_____

_____

_____

_____

_____

_____

_____

_____

_____

_____

_____

_____

_____

_____

_____

_____

_____

_____

_____

_____

_____

_____

_____

_____

_____

_____

_____

_____

Day 27: Rewards of Humility

Scripture (NASB95):

The reward of humility and the fear of the LORD are riches, honor and life.

Proverbs 22:4

Insight:

This proverb links humility (paired with fear and reverence for God) to tangible and intangible blessings. "Riches, honor, and life" summarize outcomes that people desire. While proverbs state general truths (not absolute formulas), this verse observes that those who humbly fear God often find themselves enriched in various ways. Humility positions us to receive from God and others because we're teachable and trustworthy, which can lead to success (riches) and respect (honor) over time. Moreover, "life" in a fuller sense, a meaningful, flourishing life, comes to those who live in humility before God. It's important to note the God-ward aspect ("fear of the LORD"); humility here isn't merely a social tactic, but flows from recognizing God's greatness and our dependence on Him.

Application:

If you desire the blessings of a full life, honor, or even material provision, pursue them indirectly by cultivating humility and godly reverence. Instead of aggressively pursuing status or wealth, focus on growing in character and in submission to God. Practically, put this into action by thanking God for every good thing (acknowledging Him as the source), by treating others kindly regardless of their status (showing you don't see yourself as above them), and by obeying God's word even when it cuts against your pride. Trust that in due course, God knows how to add "riches and honor" to you in the measure that is good for you. Just as Solomon, who asked for wisdom (a humble request), also received wealth and honor from the Lord. Even if earthly riches are modest, you'll gain the riches of spiritual growth and the honor of God's approval.

Reflection:

What "rewards" do you find yourself chasing most (financial security, recognition, a thriving life)? How does this proverb reframe the way to attain those things? Reflect on how you can prioritize humility and reverence for God daily (perhaps through prayer, serving in secret, or acknowledging others' contributions) and trust Him with the outcomes.

* * *

Write your reflections here:

_____

_____

_____

_____

_____

_____

_____

_____

_____

_____

_____

_____

_____

_____

_____

_____

_____

_____

_____

_____

_____

_____

_____

_____

_____

_____

Day 28: Beware of Overconfidence

Scripture (NASB95):

Therefore let him who thinks he stands take heed that he does not fall.

1 Corinthians 10:12

Insight:

Paul gives this warning after recalling how many Israelites fell into sin and judgment in the wilderness, despite being God's people. The message is clear: the moment we become overconfident in our own standing or strength, we're in spiritual danger. "Thinks he stands" describes an attitude of self-assured pride; assuming we are immune to certain temptations or beyond failure. The reality is, in our human frailty, we are always dependent on God to keep us upright. Pride can lull us into dropping our guard; then sin or failure catches us by surprise. Humility, conversely, keeps us vigilant, reminding us that we need God's grace daily. The very next verse (1 Corinthians 10:13) goes on to encourage that God provides a way of escape in temptation, but we'll only seek it if we humbly admit we need it.

Application:

Cultivate a healthy fear of God and an honest self-awareness in areas of temptation. Never assume, "I'm too strong or too spiritual ever to do X, Y, and Z," because that's precisely when the enemy can strike. Instead, acknowledge your potential to sin and stay "awake." For instance, if you have victory over a particular habit or sin, rejoice, but keep up your accountability and prayer, recognizing you still rely on God. Don't play near the fire, thinking you won't get burned; set boundaries even if you feel steady. This might mean continuing in fellowship and confession, avoiding triggers, and filling your mind with Scripture. Also, don't judge others harshly when they fall; learn from their falls and stay humble, knowing it's only by God's grace you stand.

Reflection:

Can you identify any area where you've become complacent or overconfident ("standing" in your own eyes)? Perhaps you think, "I'd never stumble in that way." How can you "take heed" in that area? What practical precautions or spiritual disciplines can you maintain to guard against a fall? Remember to pray regularly, "Lord, keep me dependent on You, and protect me from pride that would lead to a downfall."

* * *

Write your reflections here:

_____

_____

_____

_____

_____

_____

_____

_____

_____

_____

_____

_____

_____

_____

_____

_____

_____

_____

_____

_____

_____

_____

_____

_____

_____

_____

_____

Day 29: Humbly Receive God's Word

Scripture (NASB95):

Therefore, putting aside all filthiness and all that remains of wickedness, in humility receive the word implanted, which is able to save your souls.

James 1:21

Insight:

James here highlights the attitude we need to truly benefit from God's Word. We are to "receive" God's message, like fertile soil accepting a seed, but the key is the manner: *in humility*. A prideful heart will resist the Word, either by thinking we don't need it or by stubbornly holding on to sinful habits ("filthiness and wickedness"). A humble heart, however, is teachable and repentant; it welcomes God's truth even when it convicts or challenges. James likens God's Word to an implanted seed that can save and transform us, but our posture determines whether that seed takes root. Humility says, "I need God's instruction; I'm willing to be changed."

Application:

Cultivate a humble posture every time you read the Bible or hear a sermon. Practically, this means coming without an "I already know this" attitude or an agenda to justify yourself. Instead, pray beforehand, "Lord, speak to me; I'm listening and willing to learn." Be ready to put aside sinful behaviors or thoughts as the Word exposes them, essentially pulling the weeds so the seed can grow. You might start a practice of journaling what God shows you and writing down steps of obedience, which is a way of submitting to His Word. If Scripture challenges a long-held opinion or desire of yours, humility will yield to God's wisdom over your own. Remember, the goal is not just information but transformation, and that happens when a meek, open heart lets God's Word have authority.

Reflection:

How do you react when a Bible passage or sermon points out something uncomfortable or wrong in your life? Do you bristle and find excuses, or do you accept and repent? Think of one area where you've been resistant to biblical instruction. What would it look like to *humbly* receive God's implanted Word there (perhaps seeking accountability, changing a habit, or simply praying, "Lord, I submit to what You say")?

* * *

Write your reflections here:

Day 30: God's Favor on the Humble

Scripture (NASB95):

But to this one I will look, To him who is humble and contrite of spirit, and who trembles at My word.

Isaiah 66:2

Insight:

In this final chapter of Isaiah, God declares what kind of person draws His regard. It's not the one with impressive offerings or human credentials; instead, God looks with favor on the person who is humble (lowly in their own eyes), contrite in spirit (repentant and broken-hearted over sin), and who trembles at God's word (deeply respects and submits to His commands). "I will look to" can be understood as God esteeming or paying attention to that person. This powerful promise shows that our heart posture matters more to God than anything external. The Creator of the universe, whom the heavens cannot contain (Isaiah 66:1), chooses to draw near to the one who humbly recognizes their need for Him.

Application:

Make it your life's aim to be the kind of person described here. Cultivate a soft heart before God: practice regular confession of sin (contrition) and turn from it. Don't allow pride to harden you; keep an attitude that "trembles" at His word (meaning you take the Bible seriously and reverently). For example, when you read a command or a warning in Scripture, let it weigh on you enough to prompt action or change. In prayer, you might literally kneel or bow, sometimes as a physical expression of humility. Remember that nothing gets God's attention like genuine humility and reverence. When you feel insignificant or unseen, take comfort in the fact that God's eyes are on the humble. He delights to revive and dwell with those lowly in spirit (Isaiah 57:15).

Reflection:

God "looks to" the humble and contrite. Imagine God gazing at you with favor and attention. What areas of your inner life might need adjustment for this to be true of you? Do you treat His Word with reverence and obedience, or has it become casual to you? Conclude this 30-day journey by praying that Isaiah 66:2 would be a reality in your life. Ask God to work in you a continually humble, penitent, and receptive heart that He loves to bless.

* * *

Write your reflections here:

_____

_____

_____

_____

_____

_____

_____

_____

_____

_____

_____

_____

_____

_____

_____

_____

_____

_____

_____

_____

_____

_____

_____

_____

_____

_____

_____

_____

Conclusion: The Way Up Is Down

Over the past thirty days, we have walked through the tension between humility and pride—two heart postures that shape our relationship with God, our treatment of others, and the direction of our lives. Scripture has repeatedly shown that pride leads to ruin, resistance to God, and spiritual blindness, while humility draws God's favor, cultivates wisdom, and paves the way for spiritual renewal.

We've learned that humility is not weakness or self-deprecation, but a proper understanding of ourselves in light of God's greatness. It is displayed in servanthood, confession, teachability, and a Christ-centered life that seeks to elevate others rather than self. Pride, by contrast, is a delusion of self-sufficiency, a craving for glory, and a refusal to yield (always toxic to the soul).

Ultimately, this devotional has not been a call to better behavior but to more profound transformation. It is a summons to follow Jesus Christ—the One who humbled Himself to the point of death on a cross, and who is now exalted above all. In Him, humility is not just a virtue to pursue but a Person to behold. And in beholding Him, we are changed.

As you move forward:

- Let humility shape how you pray, serve, lead, and relate.

- Let Scripture remain your mirror and lifeline.

- Let Christ be your example and source of strength.

God is still looking for those who are humble and contrite of heart, who tremble at His Word (Isaiah 66:2). May that be said of you.

The way up in the kingdom of God is always down. Walk low, and Christ will be glorified in you.